The Birthday Puppy

By Jana Yankoviz Dalrymple

Illustrated by Cher Jiang

This is a work of nonfiction. No names have been changed,
no characters invented, no events fabricated.

Illustrations by Cher Jiang
Book design by Laura Moreno

ISBN: 979-8-218-12472-4

This book is dedicated to Ruth Zimmerman, whose knowledge, support, and encouragement have made my long-awaited dream a reality.

The minute I saw that lady,   I knew she was crazy about me. I also knew her husband and son would fall instantly in love with me.

I stole her heart.

She had to have me for her son Austin's fourth birthday.

She kept saying something about how I smelled. I just didn't get it.   I was a puppy, for Pete's sake! She had an interesting smell, too, but I guessed most human beings did.

We both had a lot to learn.

The lady who wanted to sell my brother and me told my lady to think about it and get back to her. My brother was a black and white Cocker Spaniel, and I was honey and white.

I knew my lady wanted ME!

There was something in her eyes. They were big and brown, just like mine!

Just like I knew she would, my lady called the next day and wanted ME. I WAS going to be the birthday puppy. I couldn't stand the excitement! I tried playing regular puppy games to keep myself busy, but the hours seemed to pass so slowly. I waited all day to go to the school where she taught and to go home with her to meet MY BOY!

At last, the moment arrived.

He was a cute little guy. He wore these glasses that were almost as big as he was. He loved me right away. I ran between his feet and he giggled and played with me. My lady even took videos of us.

I was having a ball! I felt like a movie star!

My lady knew what she wanted to name me. There was no question about it. My name was to be "Snoopy," after her favorite cartoon character.

My lady's husband came home from work and her mom came over from next door. I had a new family – my own boy, a human mom and dad, and a human grandma, too. Boy, was I a lucky dog! My new grandma said I was her "granddogger!"

My new family made a bed for me on their closed-in back porch. I called it my bedroom. It had a wooden floor that was fun to slide on. My dad said I had hairy paws, which came in really handy for sliding. My bedroom was a great place. I could hear my family talking inside, and in nice weather, they would open the big wooden doors and I could see them through the screens.

It was perfect.

The first night with my human family sure lasted a long time. I missed my puppy mom and I had trouble sleeping. I tried my best not to think about my puppy family and concentrated on a great life with my human family. I knew I would be truly happy with them!

The next morning my mom put me and my boy in her car and headed back towards the place where she had gotten me.

Oh no! Was she going to give me back? Maybe she didn't want me after all.

I was so sad. I just curled up in the corner of the box she'd put me in and wiped my puppy tears with my paw. I hoped that my mom and my boy didn't notice that I was crying. I was trying hard to be a big boy puppy, even though I didn't understand what was happening.

After a while, the car stopped and my mom showed me to a lady I had never seen before. She told the lady that I was her new granddogger.

I had another grandma - a town grandma, and now, a farm grandma!

Mom said that my boy and I were going to spend the day with her. We sure had fun playing at my farm grandma's house. I even got to experience a new thing called a "bath"! It was pretty scary at first, but, after a while, I started to enjoy it.

She said it would make me smell better. Here we went again with that smell good business! Humans sure worried about that stuff a lot.

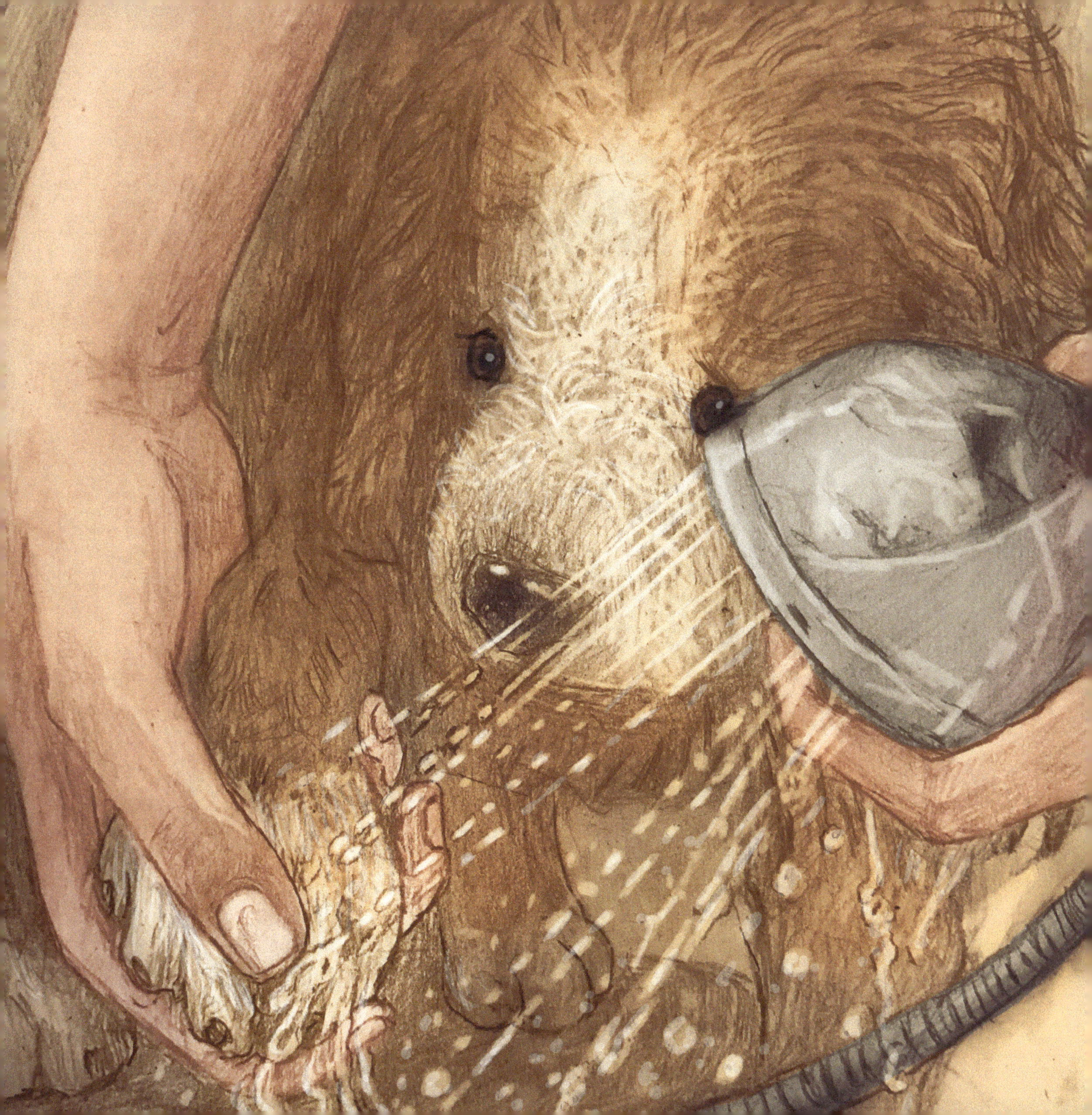

Later that day, my mom came back to my farm grandma's house and my boy and I rode back to my new home. As the days went by, I got used to being the new puppy on the block. I even got used to the humans' smell. Did you know they take a bath every day?

Usually, my boy and my town grandma stayed home with me while my mom and dad were gone to work each day, because my boy wasn't old enough for kindergarten yet. When my mom and dad came home from work, they would play with me and say how much I had grown.

I didn't feel any different!

Sometimes I'd get so excited to see my family that I'd piddle on the floor. Boy, Mom sure didn't like that! That was the first time Dad said I was a lucky dog, except when Mom was mad at me! It was ok, though, because I knew she wanted me to grow up to be a good puppy boy.

Being Austin's birthday puppy was just one of so many happy days, weeks, months, and years growing up with my boy and my human family!